First edition for the United States published
1997 by Barron's Educational Series, Inc.
Copyright © HarperCollins Publishers Ltd. 1996
Editor: Susie Elwes
Director of Photography: Michael Raggett
Photography: Tony May
Design: Schermuly Design Co., London

All inquiries should be addressed to:
Barron's Educational Series, Inc.
250 Wireless Boulevard
Hauppauge, New York 11788

First published in Great Britain in 1997

Library of Congress Catalog Card No. 97-12141

ISBN 0-7641-5049-9

Library of Congress Cataloging-in-Publication Data
Wansbrough, Henry, 1934–
        In the beginning: the story of the Old Testament / Henry
Wansbrough.
                p.   cm.
        Summary: Retells nineteen stories from the Old Testament in modern
language.
        ISBN 0-7641-5049-9
        1. Bible stories, English—O.T.   [1. Bible stories—O.T.]
I. Title.
BS551.2.W243   1997
221.9'505—dc21   97–12141
                                                                         CIP
                                                                          AC

Printed and bound in Italy

IN THE
BEGINNING

The Story of the Old Testament
Photographed as if you were there!

Henry Wansbrough

BARRON'S

Contents

Introduction

The first four stories in The Old Testament speak of God. They tell us how God made the world and how God wants humans to be in the world.

The next stories are about the people God chose, the Hebrews, Abraham, Sarah, and their family. God called Abraham and tested him. In time of famine the whole family moved into Egypt to find food. When they became slaves to the Egyptians, God rescued them through Moses, who led them through the desert. God led them to the land of Israel, the promised land. When Moses died, Joshua led the Hebrews into the promised land, where they quickly captured the city of Jericho.

Once they had settled in the land of Israel they were ruled over by wise leaders known as judges. The last judge, Samuel, chose Saul to be the first king. Saul was not a good king so Samuel chose David to take his place. David's wise son Solomon became king after him and built a great Temple to God in the city of Jerusalem.

The story of Elijah shows that the Israelites were soon disloyal to God and turned to false Gods. The great Temple in Jerusalem was destroyed and the Israelites were taken away as prisoners to Babylon. In exile in Babylon the Israelites turned back to God. In time they returned to Jerusalem and rebuilt the Temple.

The photographs in this book were taken in Israel to show the land, the people, and the animals you will find in these stories. Together they make an epic story of how God loved and shaped his people.

The Creation

In the beginning God created the world, but it was empty, shapeless, and dark. So God said, "Let there be light." And there was light and God was pleased with the light. There was water everywhere, so God made a great plan to keep the waters back and dry land appeared. God was pleased with that too. Then God made all the plants, the flowers, and fruit trees, and was pleased with them too.

In this great plan God put things that move. In the heavens God put the sun, the moon, and the stars. These were the first clocks; their movements mark the time. In the waters God put great sea monsters and slippery fish in their millions. Above the earth God put birds to fly and sing. On

the earth God put all the animals, wild and tame, even snakes and worms. And God was pleased with them all.

Finally, God made man and woman. God said, "Let us make human beings in our own image and likeness, to be caretakers of the fish in the sea, the birds in heaven, the animals wild and tame, even the snakes and worms." So they were made in God's own image and likeness, to be caretakers of the fish in the sea, the birds in heaven, the animals wild and tame, even the snakes and worms.

And God blessed them all so that they should be fruitful, increase in number, and fill the whole earth. God worked for six days. On the seventh day God rested from all work and blessed the day. Ever after, the seventh day would be dedicated to God because on this day God rested.

God called the light the day.

Adam and Eve

God formed the man from clay and breathed into this body the breath of life. God settled the man in a garden with rivers flowing through it and lush fruit trees. The man could eat the fruit of these trees. Only in the middle of the garden there was one tree, whose fruit the man must not eat.

God made all the wild animals and birds and brought them to the man. The man gave each of them a name. But the man was still lonely. So God sent him to sleep. While he was asleep, God took one of his ribs and shaped it into a woman. God brought the woman to the man and he was delighted. At last the man had a friend and companion.

Now the wily serpent asked the woman, "Did God really forbid you to eat the fruit of any of the trees?" "No," replied the woman. "Only the fruit of the tree in the middle of the garden. If we do, we will die." "You will not die!" replied the serpent. "God is just afraid that you will have knowledge of both good and evil." So she took some fruit and ate it, and gave some to the man. Suddenly they both knew that they were naked.

In the cool evening God came toward them but they were ashamed and hid in the trees. "Have you been eating from the forbidden tree?" asked God. "The woman gave me some," said the man. "The serpent tricked me into eating the fruit," said the woman.

So God cursed the serpent first. To the woman he said, "From now on you will give birth to children painfully."

To the man he said, "From now on you will have food to eat only from your own hard work."

A river flowed out of Eden to water the garden.

On the sixth day God made the animals and the human beings.

The Flood

God said to Noah, "Human beings have acted so wickedly that I am going to destroy all living things on the earth. But I will save you and your family. Build yourself a large wooden boat. Take into it a pair of every kind of animal and bird, and plenty of food."

So Noah built a boat, the ark, and took aboard a pair of every kind of animal and bird. Seven days later the waters began to flood the earth. It rained continuously for forty days and forty nights. The waters lifted the ark off the ground and it floated away over the waters. The waters rose higher and higher until even the highest mountains were submerged. Every living thing on earth was covered by water.

But God kept Noah and his animals in mind. After five months God sent a wind to dry out the earth. Little by little

Noah and his sons took the animals into the ark.

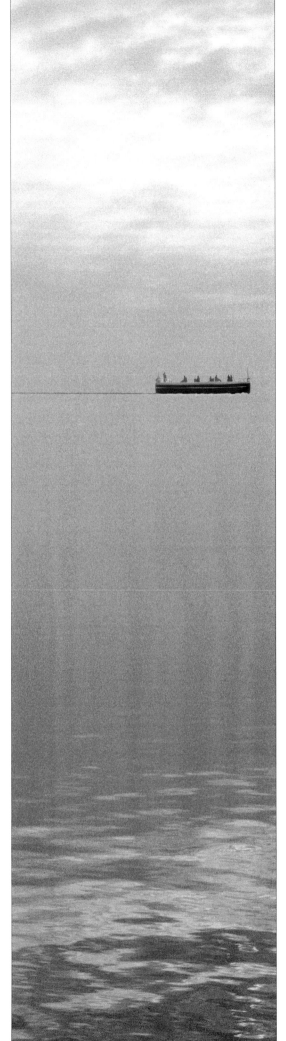

the waters went down, until the boat came to rest on the top of a mountain. The waters continued to subside and other mountaintops began to appear.

After another forty days Noah let a raven out through a window. It flew around, waiting for the waters to go away. Next he sent out a dove, but it could find nowhere to perch and came back. Noah waited a week and sent the dove out again. It came back with a freshly picked olive leaf. Noah realized that the mountains and hills were above the water. He waited another week and sent the dove out a third time. It did not come back.

Noah opened the hatch of the boat and looked out. The surface of the earth was dry! So Noah came out with all his family and the animals and birds. God blessed Noah and his family. "Never again shall I destroy all living things," said God. "This is a promise to you all. As a sign of my promise I am putting a rainbow in the sky. Whenever the rainbow appears in the sky, it will remind you of my promise."

The waters rose until they covered the mountains. Only the ark floated on the flood.

After five months in the ark there was enough dry land for Noah and the animals to leave the ark.

The Tower of Babel

At that time people all over the world spoke the same language. Some people wandered a long way to find new land. They settled in a valley in the land of Babylon. They said to one another, "Come on, let's build a city!" In those days people used stone to build houses, held together by cement made out of crumbled stone. But in Babylon there was no stone, only sand and mud. So they said, "As there is no stone we will make bricks out of mud and harden them by baking them in a fire." For cement between the bricks they used tar. In the middle of the city they decided to build a tower right up to heaven. They thought, "Everyone will see the tower reaching up to heaven and it will make us famous. Together we will build a tower and it will keep us all together as the people of the tower."

When they started work, God came to see the city and the tower they were building. God thought, "They are so pleased with themselves that they will believe they can do anything they want to do. There will be no limit to their plans. I will go and muddle their language so that they will not understand one another. Then they will not be able to work together and they will scatter and find somewhere else to live."

So God muddled their words. They could not understand one another, their speech sounded like babble. They stopped building the city and went into different places. That is why people in different countries speak different languages. The babble is the reason why it is called the Tower of Babel.

The people began to build a tower to reach heaven.

The Call of Abraham

Abraham's family lived in Ur. This was a great city, with grand temples. It was busy with merchants and rich nobles in their chariots. The family left Ur and settled far to the north in another trading town, Haran.

One day God said to Abraham, "Leave your friends and neighbors and your father's house and go to a land I will show you. I shall make you a great nation. I shall bless you and make your descendants like dust on the ground. When people succeed in counting the specks of dust on the ground, then they will be able to count your descendants too!"

Abraham trusted God's promise. He gave up his comfortable life and set off for Canaan, taking everything he had with him. He lived in a rough tent. The country is hilly and stony. Abraham camped outside the towns, on the edge of the desert, wherever he could find grazing for his sheep and goats. Wherever he went he made a shrine and prayed to God. But he still had no children.

One year there was a famine. Abraham went across the desert to Egypt, where the River Nile provides plenty of water. Every year it floods, leaving rich river mud, or silt, on the fields, which quickly produces a crop. In Egypt, Abraham found food for his sheep and cattle.

Now Sarah, his wife, was very beautiful. The King of Egypt saw her and wanted to steal her away from Abraham. But God sent disease and sickness on the king. So the King of Egypt let Sarah go. He was afraid that he had angered Abraham's God. So he gave Abraham gifts of sheep and cattle. In this way God blessed Abraham.

Abraham left the city of Haran and led his followers to the land of Canaan.

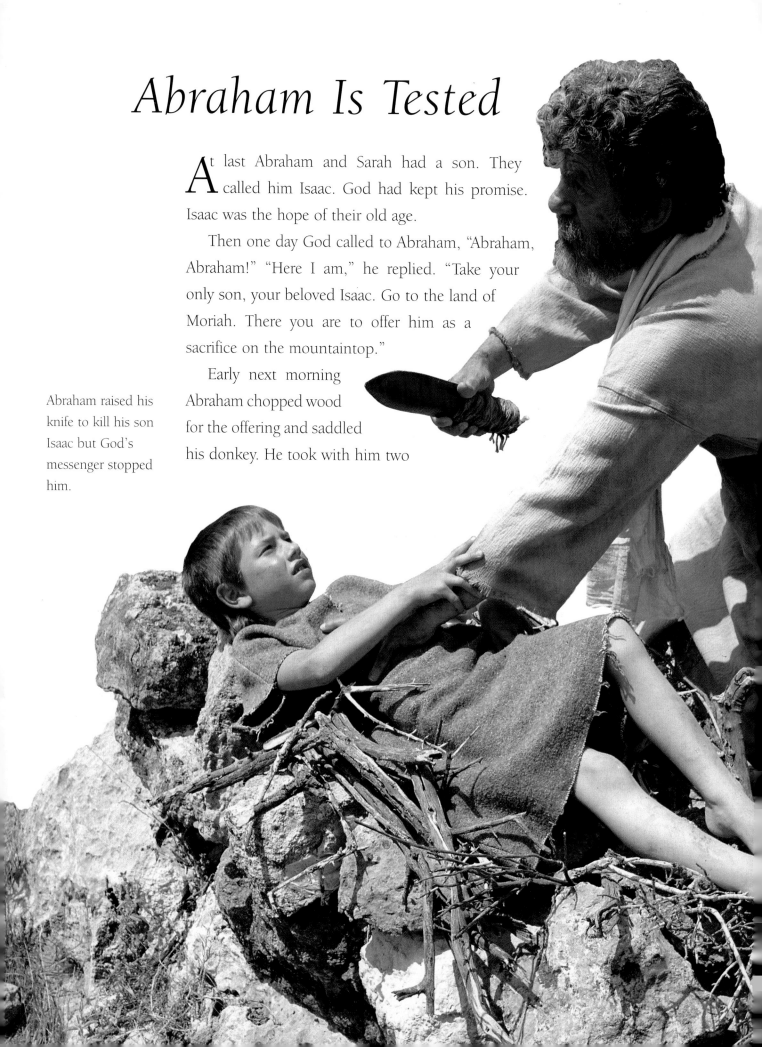

Abraham Is Tested

At last Abraham and Sarah had a son. They called him Isaac. God had kept his promise. Isaac was the hope of their old age.

Then one day God called to Abraham, "Abraham, Abraham!" "Here I am," he replied. "Take your only son, your beloved Isaac. Go to the land of Moriah. There you are to offer him as a sacrifice on the mountaintop."

Early next morning Abraham chopped wood for the offering and saddled his donkey. He took with him two

Abraham raised his knife to kill his son Isaac but God's messenger stopped him.

young men and his son Isaac and started on the journey. On the third day Abraham saw the place in the distance and said to the young men, "Stay here with the donkey. The boy and I are going over there. We will be back soon."

Abraham gave Isaac the wood to carry, but he himself carried the pot of fire and the knife. They walked in silence. Then Isaac said to his father, "Father!" "Yes, my son," he replied. "The fire and the wood are here but where is the lamb for the offering?" Abraham replied, "God himself will provide the lamb." The two walked on together in silence.

When they arrived at the place, Abraham built an altar and arranged the wood on it. Then he took his son and lifted him onto the altar on top of the wood. He stretched out his hand and held the knife ready to kill his son.

Then the Angel of the Lord called to Abraham, "Abraham, Abraham!" "Here I am," he replied. "Do not raise your hand against the boy. Now I know that you trust God. You have not refused your own beloved son."

Abraham looked up, and saw a ram caught in a thicket by the horns. So Abraham offered the ram instead of his son.

The Angel of the Lord called again, "Because you have not refused me your own beloved son, I will bless you. I will make your descendants as many as the stars in heaven and the grains of sand on the seashore."

Travelers carried little pots of hot embers so they could easily start a cooking fire.

19

Joseph Sold Into Slavery

Jacob, the son of Isaac, loved Joseph more than all his other sons.

Joseph's ten elder brothers were jealous of him. His father loved his youngest son more than all the others, and made him a special tunic with long sleeves and many colors. One night Joseph had a dream that they were all in a field, harvesting. Joseph's sheaf of corn stood upright and the sheaves of all the brothers bowed down to it. He told his brothers his dream, and that only made them more jealous.

When Joseph was seventeen he went to find his brothers, who were away from home looking after the sheep. They recognized his tunic from afar and decided to get rid of him. When he got to them, they stripped him of his tunic and threw him into an empty well. Soon afterwards some merchants came by on their way to Egypt. They were carrying goods to sell. So the brothers sold Joseph to them as a slave and took his tunic back to their father. They smeared blood on it and pretended that wild beasts had eaten Joseph. His father was heartbroken.

In Egypt the merchants sold Joseph to Potiphar, one of the king's officials. Potiphar's wife found Joseph very attractive. One day, when Potiphar was out, she asked Joseph to lie with her but he refused. In her fury she tore off his garment and pretended that he had attacked her. Nobody believed Joseph, and he was thrown into prison.

One of Joseph's fellow prisoners was the king's cupbearer. He had a dream one night and Joseph explained it: the cupbearer was to get his old job back. And so he did. Then the king had a dream: seven fat cows came up from the River Nile. Seven thin cows followed and ate them up. The king was worried but his cupbearer said he knew someone who could explain the dream. So they gave Joseph a quick bath and clean clothes and rushed him to the king. Joseph explained that there would be seven good harvests followed by seven bad harvests that would bring famine. The king was so impressed that he asked Joseph to manage the corn supply.

Joseph became rich and important. His father and brothers came to join him in Egypt, when they too ran out of food.

Joseph was thrown into a well before he was sold as a slave.

Moses

Many years passed and the Egyptians made the Hebrews work as slaves to build their cities. The Egyptian King, or Pharaoh, ordered all Hebrew boy babies to be killed at birth. But one, called Moses, escaped. His mother put him in a basket that floated, hidden by reeds on the River Nile, just where the king's daughter bathed. The princess heard the baby crying and adopted him as her own. Moses' sister, Miriam, who had been hiding nearby, offered to find a nurse for the baby. The nurse she found was their own mother.

When Moses grew up, God gave him the task of setting his people free. One day he saw an Egyptian official treating one of the Hebrews brutally, so he killed him and hid the body.

Moses was hidden in a basket, floating on the river.

The Hebrews were slaves and worked very hard building new cities with bricks.

The Egyptians soon found out and Moses fled to the desert. There he became a shepherd. One day, as he was looking after the sheep, he saw a bush ablaze without being burned up. He went over to see how this was possible, and a voice told him to take off his sandals because he was in a holy place.

The voice was the voice of God, who had called Abraham and promised to protect him. Now God sent Moses to tell the King of Egypt to set the Hebrews free. The king refused and was so angry that he made sure the Hebrews worked even harder in their slavery.

Moses ran away from the Egyptians and became a shepherd in Midian.

Passover

The Hebrews were told to paint their doorposts with blood, so the Angel would know their houses and pass over them without harm.

God told Moses to go back to the king and command him to let the Hebrews go. Moses went to the king but the king refused to do as Moses commanded. Moses threw his wooden staff to the ground and it turned into a snake. But the king would not let the Hebrews go. So God sent plagues upon the Egyptians. The river water turned to blood. Frogs jumped around inside their houses. Mosquitoes and flies stung everyone. Their cattle all died. Everyone suffered with boils on their skin. Hail storms flattened the crops. There was a whole day without sunlight, when Egypt was in darkness. With each plague the king agreed to let the Hebrews go but as soon as the plague stopped he changed his mind.

Nothing could persuade the king to free the Hebrews. Finally, the Angel of the Lord slew the eldest child of every family, human and animal. To ward off this final, terrible plague, the Hebrews painted blood on the doorposts of their houses, as the Angel had told them to do. Before they left Egypt they had a special feast to thank the Angel for passing over their houses and God for setting them free.

Each year this special feast is repeated to remind the people of God's care for them. They eat lamb, unleavened bread, bitter herbs, and red wine to remind them of the blood that was shed. The youngest boy asks the eldest man to explain the story.

At Passover roast lamb and unleavened bread are eaten.

At Mount Sinai

God led the Hebrews through the desert, going in front of them as a column of cloud by day and as a pillar of fire by night. The Egyptians chased after them. The Hebrews found their way blocked by a stretch of water. God sent a strong wind, which blew on the water, and the Hebrews were able to walk through it. But when the Egyptian chariots tried to cross, they got stuck in the mud. The wind stopped blowing, the horses panicked, and the Egyptians drowned.

The Hebrews in the desert wandered with their flocks from well to well.

Life in the desert was hard for the Hebrews. They had little to eat and very little to drink. So they rebelled against God and the Laws he had given them. They collected all their gold and jewelry, melted it down, and made a golden statue of a calf. They danced and sang around the statue and worshipped it as their new god.

Moses was given God's commandments on Mount Sinai. He was away so long, his people thought he was dead and began to worship a golden calf.

Moses was furious, but he begged God to forgive the Hebrews. Moses went up the mountain to be alone with God for forty days and forty nights. There God appeared to him in a cloud. God forgave the people and promised to love them if they would love him and keep his Laws.

The Walls of Jericho

When the Hebrews had wandered in the desert for forty years Moses died. He had chosen Joshua to be the new leader. Joshua crossed the Jordan River and the Hebrews entered the promised land.

In front of them was the great city of Jericho. Joshua sent two men ahead to spy on the city. They went to the house of a woman called Rahab. The King of Jericho sent a message to Rahab: "Send out those men who have come to spy on the city." But she let them escape from a window in the city wall. Then Jericho shut and barricaded its gates against the Hebrew people called Israelites.

God said to Joshua, "Look, I am putting Jericho at your mercy." Joshua summoned the priests and said, "Take the Ark of the Covenant, the sacred box that contains the Laws and shows that God is with us. Let seven priests carry seven ram's horn trumpets ahead of the Ark." To the people he said, "Do not raise a war cry. Keep silent."

So the seven priests, blowing their seven ram's horn trumpets, marched around the city and went back to camp. The people marched with them in silence. This happened for six days. On the seventh day they marched around the city seven times. At the seventh time, as the priests blew their horns, Joshua said, "Raise the war cry, for God has given us the city."

The Israelites raised a mighty war cry and the walls of Jericho fell down. They stormed into the city and killed every living thing. Rahab and her family were spared.

The King of Jericho ordered the city gates to be shut and his warriors got ready to defend the walls.

The priest sounds the shofar, or ram's horn.

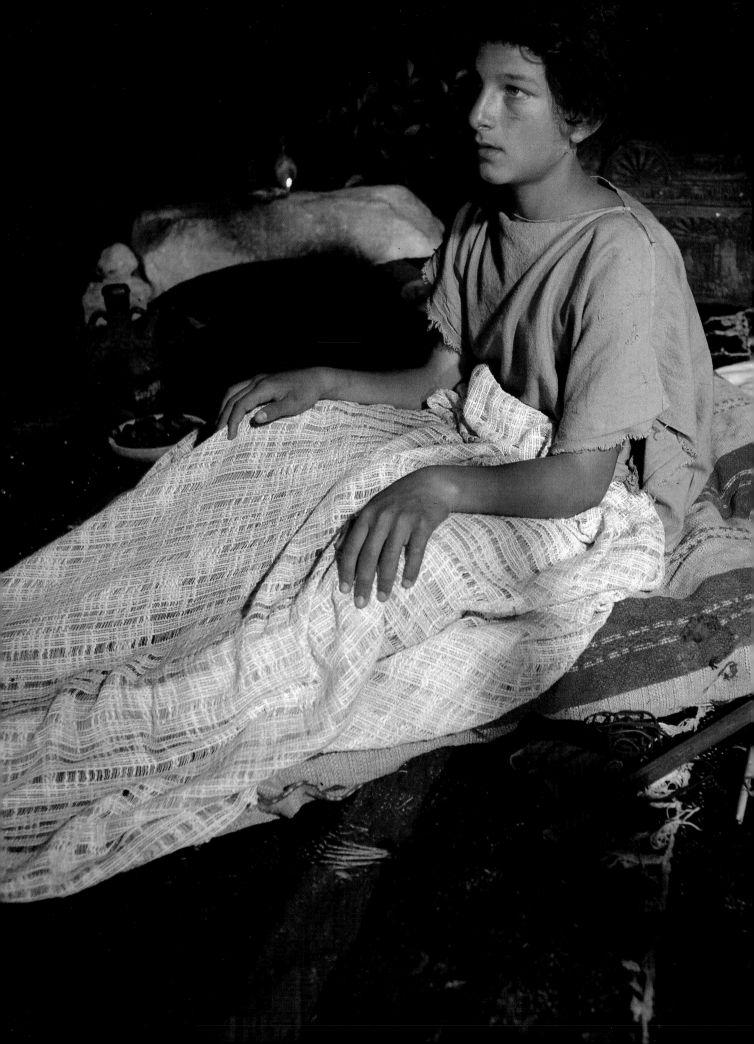

The Call of Samuel

Now the boy Samuel was serving the old priest Eli in the House of the Lord. One evening, Eli was lying down in his room. The lamp of God had not yet gone out, and Samuel was lying down in the sanctuary, beside the Ark of the Lord.

The Lord called to him, "Samuel, Samuel!" "Here I am," replied Samuel. He ran to Eli and said, "Here I am, as you called me." Eli said, "I did not call. Go back and lie down." So Samuel went and lay down.

Samuel slept in front of the Ark in the sanctuary.

Again the Lord called to him, "Samuel, Samuel!" Again he went to Eli. Again he was told to go back and lie down in the sanctuary.

The Lord called a third time. Samuel got up, went to Eli, and said, "Here I am, as you called me." Then Eli understood that the Lord was calling the child. He said to Samuel, "Go back and lie down, and if someone calls, say, 'Speak, Lord, for your servant is listening'."

A light was left burning in the sanctuary.

The Lord then came and stood by, calling as he had done before, "Samuel, Samuel!" Samuel answered, "Speak, Lord, for your servant is listening."

The Lord then said to Samuel, "Tell Eli that I condemn his family for ever. He knows that his own sons have been cursing God, and he has not corrected them."

Samuel lay there till morning. He was afraid to give Eli the message. But Eli called him, "Samuel, come here." So Samuel had to give him God's message.

Samuel grew up and the Lord was with him.

David and Goliath

The Philistines gathered their troops for war and came up from the coast into the hill country to terrorize the Israelites. The Israelites also gathered their troops. The armies were encamped on the high ground, on opposite sides of a valley.

A champion came out from among the Philistines to challenge the Israelites to single combat. The Philistine was ten feet tall and his name was Goliath.

Goliath was the giant champion of the Philistines. He was brought down by a stone from a shepherd's simple sling.

A young shepherd boy called David came to visit his elder brothers in the Israelite army, bringing them food from home. While he was talking to them, Goliath came out and made his usual speech. All the Israelites ran away in terror. David asked what the prize would be for killing Goliath, but his elder brothers thought he was being boastful and they were cross with him.

Then David went up to the Israelite king, Saul. "I will go and fight this Philistine," he said.

Saul replied, "You can't go and fight him. You are only a boy." But David persuaded Saul. He said he had fought off lions and bears when they attacked his sheep. Saul gave David his own armor but it was too big for the boy.

So David went out with nothing but his stick, his slingshot, and five smooth stones. Goliath taunted him, "Am I a dog, for you to come at me with a stick?"

"I come to you in the name of the Lord God of Israel," replied David. He took out a stone, hurled it, and struck Goliath on the head. The giant fell down dead. David cut off his head with Goliath's own sword.

David used Goliath's own sword to cut off his head. The Philistines ran away.

David and Saul

Samuel, now a Judge of Israel, anointed Saul to be the first King of Israel.

David came back to Saul with Goliath the Philistine's head in his hands. Saul immediately took him into his army. He made him commander of the army, and David was successful in all his battles. Soon people were singing, "Saul has killed thousands, but David tens of thousands." Saul became madly jealous.

Saul's son, Jonathan, admired David. They became close friends and were like brothers. Saul fell into moods of black despair and rage at David's success. David was a fine musician, and tried to soothe Saul by playing gentle music to him. It was no good. Twice in his frenzy Saul tried to pin David to the wall with his spear.

David decided to leave the court and hide in the caves of the desert. Saul chased him with his soldiers. One day Saul went into a cave to relieve himself, not realizing that David was hiding deep in the same cave. Saul took off his heavy cloak and while he squatted down, David crept up and cut off a piece of the cloak. Saul put on the cloak again and left. When he was at a safe distance, David cried out, "My lord king! Look at the piece of cloth in my hand! I could have killed you, but I was too loyal." Saul realized that he had been wrong about David, and the two became friends. But Saul soon became jealous again.

So David left Saul's court forever and set up his own army. He protected the country people from thieves on the roads and gangs of robbers in the desert. By protecting people he made many friends. Later, when Saul and Jonathan were killed in battle, the nobles came and offered the crown to David. David was heartbroken at the death of his friend Jonathan. He accepted the crown and was anointed King of the Israelites.

David cut off the corner of Saul's cloak, to show Saul that he could have killed him.

Saul's son, Jonathan, and David became good friends.

Absalom's Rebellion

David was king for many years. He grew old and weak. His ambitious eldest son, Absalom, decided to make himself king. As Absalom and his army advanced on Jerusalem, King David withdrew from the city to avoid fighting in the streets. Absalom chased his father and his army away from the hills near Jerusalem toward the Jordan Valley. There, in the forests, a great battle took place.

David was too old to join in the fighting. As he sent the army into battle, he told every man, "Do not harm Absalom!" Then he sat and waited.

Absalom's army was defeated. Absalom fled, riding a mule. He passed under a thick oak tree and his head got stuck in the branches. The mule went on, leaving him hanging there. One of the soldiers reported this to David's trusted general, Joab. Joab took three spears and thrust them into Absalom's heart as he hung there. Joab's bodyguard finally killed Absalom.

How should they tell David? Joab sent one of the soldiers ahead with the news for David. The soldier knew David would be heartbroken and took a long road back. As David sat and waited, the lookout saw a lone man running towards them. "That is good news," said David. "Defeated soldiers come in groups." The man arrived and told David of the victory, but he also told him that Absalom was dead.

David burst into tears. He went up to his room. When the army came back they could all hear him weeping and crying out, "My son, Absalom! Absalom, my son, my son!" They crept back like a defeated army.

Absalom fled but was trapped by branches and speared to death.

Solomon's Temple

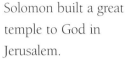

Solomon built a great temple to God in Jerusalem.

King David died, and Solomon became king. He was known as a wise man. One day two women stood before him. The first woman said, "We live in the same house, and each of us has had a child. In the night her baby died. So, while I was asleep, she put the dead baby in my arms and took from me my living baby." They argued about it, each saying that the living baby was her own. "Bring me a sword," said King Solomon. "Cut the child in the middle and give half to each woman." One of the women agreed, but the real mother cried out, "No, my lord, don't harm the baby. Give her the child alive." "Give the child to the woman who has protected it from harm," ruled Solomon, "for she is his true mother." After this, people came from all over the world to ask his advice.

In the inner sanctuary
were two cherubim,
carved from olive
wood.

King Solomon was also rich. He bought and sold chariots and horses to the neighboring kings. The Queen of the South came to see him with rich gifts and marvelled at his wealth and his wisdom. Jerusalem was a market for traders bringing spices on camel trains from India and further east. Solomon had a great fleet of ships, bringing ivory and apes from Africa. All Solomon's drinking cups were made of gold and he had a great ivory throne, decorated with gold.

King Solomon built a great temple to the Lord. He summoned skilled craftsmen to decorate it. These craftsmen worked carving stone and rare cedar and juniper. In front of the temple was a cedar wood altar, covered with gold. Two great winged cherubim were carved and covered with gold to guard the holiest room. The temple took seven years to build.

When the building was finished, all the people came to see the priests bring in the Ark, the most holy box in which God's Laws were kept. As they entered, a cloud filled the temple, showing that God had taken over the temple as his own. It was the sign of God's presence among his people. Solomon killed 22,000 oxen and 120,000 sheep and the people had enough food to feast for a whole week of celebrations.

Elijah and the Priests of Baal

Elijah asked for the wood to be soaked with water three times.

Ahab, King of Israel, married Jezebel, the daughter of a pagan priest from another country where they worshipped the God Baal. She brought with her from home four hundred priests of Baal. So the prophet Elijah arranged a competition against them on Mount Carmel.

All the people assembled and Elijah called out, "Make up your minds whether the Lord or Baal is your God." But the people stood there in silence.

So Elijah continued, "Tell the prophets of Baal to prepare a bull for sacrifice and I shall prepare another bull. We will not set fire to them, but the God who sends fire on the sacrifice is truly God." The prophets of Baal prepared their bull on the altar. From early morning till midday they danced around it, crying, "O Baal, answer us!" Elijah made fun of them, "Call louder," he said, "He is a God. Perhaps he is busy, or asleep, or away on a journey." So they shouted louder and slashed themselves with knives and spears to attract their God.

Midday passed, and they raved on until the time of the evening sacrifice. But there was no answer, no voice, no sign of attention. Then Elijah called to the people, "Come over here." He repaired the altar of God, which had been destroyed, and laid the bull on it. Then he told them to fill four jars of water and pour them out on the altar. They did this, repeated it, and did it a third time, until water was flowing all around the altar. Then Elijah prayed, "Lord God of Abraham, Isaac and Jacob, show that you are really God."

At that, fire fell and ate up the offering and the wood and even the water around the altar. When the people saw this they all fell down and worshipped. "The Lord is God," they cried, "The Lord is God." "Then seize the prophets of Baal," cried Elijah. "Don't let one of them escape."

The people worshipped a false God, Baal.

Elijah called on God
to set his altar alight.

Sacking Jerusalem

Jehoiachin was eighteen years old when he became king in Jerusalem. Within a few months he rebelled against the great king, Nebuchadnezzar, King of Babylon, who ruled many kings. So Nebuchadnezzar's army advanced on Jerusalem and captured it. They took back to Babylon all the gold and silver treasures from the temple. They also took with them all the nobles and all the blacksmiths and metal workers, so that there was no one left to lead a revolt or to make any weapons for it either.

King Jehoiachin was taken as a prisoner to Babylon. His uncle was put on his throne in Jerusalem. But within ten years he too had revolted. So Nebuchadnezzar and the Babylonians returned. Their siege of Jerusalem lasted for eighteen months and there was no food left for anyone in the city to eat. One night the King of Jerusalem and his bodyguard escaped in the dark. The Babylonians caught them. They slaughtered the king's sons before his eyes. Then they burned out his eyes and took him away in chains to Babylon.

The Babylonians destroyed the city of Jerusalem. They burned down all the splendid buildings, the temple, the royal palace, and all the houses. Stone by stone they took down the massive walls of Jerusalem, and left it ruined. The people were taken as slaves to Babylon.

Jerusalem was burned and the people were taken away as slaves.

The Babylonians destroyed the city of Jerusalem.

Babylon

In Babylon one of the exiles from Jerusalem wrote a poem beginning, "By the rivers of Babylon we sat and wept, as we remembered Zion. If I ever forget you, Jerusalem, let my right hand shrivel up." All the time they thought only of the splendor of Jerusalem and its temple on Mount Zion. They were prisoners in a great foreign city, with pagan Gods and temples. People prayed to the sun and the moon. So the exiles just felt homesick and abandoned. They pictured the ruined city and wrote,

> "Children who used to eat only the best,
> now lie dying in the streets.
>
> Those who used to wear fine clothes,
> now claw at the rubbish heaps."

The only thing they could do was to

In exile the Jews tried to keep God's Laws and worship on the Sabbath day.

The city of Babylon was the center of a great empire.

44

worship God, keep his Laws and remember the festivals of thanksgiving. They told each other the stories of God's help to them in earlier times. This reminded them that once before God had saved them from slavery in Egypt. In his care for his people, Israel, God sent them messengers to comfort them. One messenger, Ezekiel, explained that they were like dead bones lying scattered along a valley. Soon God would breathe over them. At the breath of God they would put on flesh and skin and come to life again as a great nation. The temple would be rebuilt, more splendid than before its destruction.

Finally, after seventy years of exile in Babylon, they were released and went back to Jerusalem. Slowly and with hard work they began to rebuild their beloved city.

They collected all their writings about God together, to read and learn.